CONTENTS

Greetings. This book consists of a series of articles dealing with a solution to help end the racial, religious, and political tensions we're experiencing in the U.S. and around the world. The articles were written to be placed onto a website as separate links, but meant to be read in sequence. The website, as explained therein the articles, is also meant to be the Central Headquarters for all involved in the intended grass roots movement. Please keep this in mind as you read through it all, including the Epilog – if you wish to be part of the exciting solution rather than the ever-worsening problems.

I dedicate these writings - which consists
of my dream to end racial, religious and political
tensions by peaceably forming New Eden
and other new countries within the U.S.
and abroad - to my 3 children who I have
always and will always love unconditionally

-Dad-

Greetings and WELCOME to the website that offers the SOLUTION to help end racial, religious and political tensions and conflicts in the U.S. and other countries around the world and enables YOU to play a VITAL ROLE in bringing about such peace.

Everyone reading this should know there are huge racial, religious, lingual, cultural and even political differences that have reached tinder box proportions amongst us Americans and citizens of other countries worldwide - causing everything from protests to riots, mass shootings, bombings and other acts of terrorism, genocide, and civil wars. Look at all the acts of violence, lootings, property damage, destruction and protests going on in the U.S. and around the world as a result of the senseless tragic killing of black male George Floyd by a white police officer in Minneapolis on 5/25/20; as well as the long-standing disputes and unrest in Israel and the Middle East, Africa, Europe, Hispaniola, and recent occurrences in U.S. cities such as Portland, Kenosha Wisconsin, New York, Atlanta, Seattle, Baltimore, Dallas, Ferguson Missouri and San Bernardino California. The Trump impeachment proceedings and 2020 election proved the U.S. is also politically fractured beyond repair. The name "UNITED States" has become an oxymoron that people mock worldwide. With two primary political parties, Democrats and Republicans will never get along and work together to fully support any president. Staunch Republican citizens view Democrats as being predominantly comprised of women who are man-hating "fem-fascists," minorities who hate "white man" and "white man's system" but love white women and want open borders, LGBTQs, and white men who have been emasculated by women, minorities, and LGBTQs, and, all of whom are brainwashed by Satan, anti-Christian anti-Bible immoral illogical free-government-handouts-for-all, radical left wing liberal hate mongers. Staunch Democrat citizens view Republicans as predominantly racist old white male Evangelical Christian hypocrites who want the rich getting richer and the poor poorer, and white women who are "trailer park trash" traitors to their sex, and, all of whom are brainwashed by "the church" and Bible, anti other religions, closed-minded self-righteous fear mongering right wing conservative ignorant rednecks. Several prominent political figures from both parties have expressed concern the U.S. Republic form of government is no longer feasible due to the ever increasing divisiveness. They are correct. For many years now, government and other leaders have been trying to program citizens into believing that living in diversity is good for a country and makes a country stronger and we all just need to get along, yet relations KEEP GETTING WORSE and people are fed up. Why? Well, because it's NORMAL for people to be partial to their own. Being partial is NOT being "racist". Racism is a harboring of at least ill feelings towards other races. It's simply human nature for people to prefer to befriend and live with those who they share the most in common with, just as in the adage and fact of nature overall: "birds of a feather flock together." So, what is the solution? To answer, we must first unprogram ourselves from all the lies by opening our minds to logic, facts, and truths.

"Every Kingdom divided against itself is brought to desolation, and every city or house divided against itself will not stand." (Quoting Jesus in Matthew 12:25). For peace and unity, the ONLY solution is to live in SEPARATE Kingdoms and houses.

Even one of the most popular movies of all time, Avatar, based its underlying theme on the premise that no matter where it is, people of different races must live separate from each other in their own lands and respect those boundaries in order to have peace between the races.

All around the world, countless millions of people recognize things are very wrong and think and talk in private about their desires to live separately with people of their own kind, and even wish they could form their own independent country with a new or autonomous government. New countries and governments CAN and DO get created. The United States is a prime example. More recent examples are found with South Sudan, Kosovo, Serbia, Montenegro, and Iraq. Plus let's not forget the breaking up of the former Soviet Union into 15 independent states by the end of 1991.

In the Bible, God actually commands separation, but "Christian leaders" intentionally neglect to tell us that fact for fear of being labeled anti- establishment, politically incorrect, or racist. All the scriptures dealing with separation are quoted and/or listed in the Living in Diversity article on this site. It's a MUST-READ article even for non-Christians because it explains why separation is also the only logical and viable solution, and gives ALL readers the opportunity to discuss it on one of the chat links of this site.

When there are so many countries with diversity having racial, religious and political problems, what prevents them from fairly dividing up the land and resources so the discontented can form their own countries and governments while the contented live in an already established part the existing country's land? After all, a country boils down to really being only land and its citizens. So when its citizens become divisive through too much diversity, the ONLY feasible solution is a peaceful separation by doling out appropriately fair amounts of land to those citizens who wish to live with their own people. Any citizens who are officials within the government of a country who would refuse to allow fellow citizens to have their own land to form their own new country and government for the sake of peace, would only be selfish and greedy and not concerned about the best interests of the citizens who are at odds, or the country as a whole as it continues to suffer.

Since so many people around the world have lost faith in existing governments, also proposed on this site is a completely innovative government system that current troubled countries and any newly forming countries' supporters and prospective citizens can enjoy implementing now. (Read the ADAM Government System link). Additionally, participants of this site can have fun proposing other government systems too. (Read the "HOW TO" link for details).

With Joe Biden and Kamala Harris winning this 2020 election, and over 70 million Republicans feeling so dejected and angry about losing to a Democrat Party that apparently wants to take the U.S. to a Socialist society, Republicans should CERTAINLY want to GET INVOLVED with forming new countries. Remaining depressed and complaining accomplishes NOTHING. Channel those emotions into ACTIONS by getting MOTIVATED to JOIN IN NOW! Republicans are hard workers and CAN get this DONE!

The Main Office has designated this site as its worldwide "Central Headquarters" because it enables discontented people all around the world the venue to bring their private discussions, thoughts and dreams to this public forum in order to effect the solution within the U.S. and their respective countries and turn the talk into actual coordinated movements. Simply by participating and/or supporting this site, YOU become an INTEGRAL PART of this Central Headquarters to End Racial, Religious and Political Tensions, Form New Countries, and New Eden. In other words, this site is YOUR Central Headquarters. Utilize its links. Propose a new country and/or government system and/or campaign to be a King, Queen, President, or other Leader. Chat and express your ideas and opinions, or simply read what others have to say. Enjoy yourself!

For those people who think forming new countries and governments can't be accomplished, or that doing such peaceful separations is not the solution, please read the following links in order and learn a lot more.

NOW is the time to bring the talk and dreams to wonderful realities.

Let's ALL help end racial, religious and political tensions NOW for the sake of love and peace amongst us and our children.

Dreams DO come true!

Although this article is based primarily on Christianity and the Bible, it also appeases all religions and atheists by using common sense logic. Please read it all the way through to understand why we have racial and religious tensions worldwide, and why separation is the only solution.

We routinely hear from our preachers, politicians, government officials, teachers, and corporate mass media that: "living in diversity is good for us" and "diversity is what makes this country great." But living in racial, religious and lingual diversity is AGAINST God's commands and purpose in His creating the diversity amongst us. Even though concerns continue to grow along the lines of increasing racial, cultural and religious divisions and violence, illegal immigrants, foreign refugees and legal immigrants who speak other languages and/or are of religions other than the existing majority; - the government, mass media, religious leaders, etc., keep insisting we must accept diversity and not speak out against it. However, EVERY country in this world that has racial, religious and/or cultural and lingual diversity is SUFFERING anything from mild racisms to outright civil wars and even acts of genocide. Being that the FACT and TRUTH is every country with such diversity is suffering from that diversity, that means our governments, mass media, etc., are LYING TO US. But besides current events and factual histories to prove such diversity is NOT good for a country, let's see what God says. Let's allow God via the Bible to give us instructions rather than listening to, and accepting, the false teachings and errant ways of man.

In the New Testament, Acts 17:26-27, we are told: "He [God] has made from one blood EVERY RACE of men to dwell on all the face of the earth, and has determined their preappointed times and the BOUNDARIES of their dwellings, so that they should seek the Lord in the hope that they might grope for Him and find Him." Most Bible translations use the word "nation" instead of "race" because "race" is a modern-day term which did not exist at the time the first English translation was done. But the Greek word used in the oldest scriptures we know of, is "ethnos", for which the primary definition is "race". (See the Strong's Exhaustive Concordance and others). We use the English words ethnic and ethnicity in the same manner of describing the racial aspect of people. According to Strong's, EVERY time we see the word "nations" used throughout the New Testament, it's actually "race(s)" (ethnos). And in the Old Testament, words such as "nation(s)", "families", "people" and "tribe(s)" are used to mean "race(s)" in various scriptures. So you can see that God gave separate boundaries for the different races. That scripture also tells us God "made" every race of mankind, and that we are not physically different looking due to any kind of evolution or adaptation to our environments.

God made us different looking for a reason. God INITIALLY created man to be just "one" race (Acts 17:26), and to speak only one language: "The whole earth had ONE LANGUAGE" (Gen. 11:1). But all that CHANGED at the Tower of Babel incident. God said: "Indeed the people are one AND they all have one language... Come, let Us go down and there confuse their language that they may not understand one another's speech. So the Lord SCATTERED THEM abroad from there over the face of the earth" (Gen. 11:6-8). From "one" race and language, the people: "were SEPARATED into their lands...according to their LANGUAGES...according to their RACES" (Gen. 10:5, 20, 31 & 32). God does NOT want us to be "one" anymore; which is WHY He changed, scattered and separated us, and gave us "boundaries". (Also see Deut. 32:8). God wants us to "grope for Him and find Him" (Acts 17:27) as SEPARATED races and countries of people. When man was one race and language, they were able to unite together as one and became prideful, corrupted, and displeasing to God as one entire nation of people of the world. But because God promised to never destroy every living thing again (Gen. 8:21 & 9:8-12), He instead chose to punish man by CAUSING DIFFERENCES amongst us PHYSICALLY (by race) AND SOCIALLY (by language), and separating and scattering us BY RACE AND LANGUAGE "over the face of the earth". God then gave commandments for all who believe in Him to obey.

God COMMANDED SEPARATION from other races and religions, and also to NOT intermarry with them. (Please READ: Ex. 33:16; Lev. 20:24; Deut. 7:1-6 & 16; Josh. 23:11-13; Ezra 9:1-3 & 12 and 10:10-11; Neh. 9:2, 13:1-3 & 23-27; Dan. 2:43; 2 Cor. 6:14-17; and Jude 5-8 for scriptural examples. Latter Day Saints please also read

Alma 5:57 and 3:6, 9 & 14; 3 Nephi 15:19-21; Moses 7:8 & 22; and Articles of Faith 6 & 8). Contrary to man's lies, GOD NEVER WITHDREW OR CHANGED THOSE COMMANDS OF US. We are also shown God's identical ways in other creations.

God created every fruit, herb, seed, insect, bird, fowl, fish, reptile, animal, etc., to multiply: "AFTER ITS OWN KIND" (See Gen. 1:11-25, Lev. 11:14-29, etc.). This means apples produce apples and oranges produce oranges even though both are "fruit". They don't interlive and interbreed. Salmon live and breed with Salmon and produce salmon, and tuna with tuna, etc., even though all are "fish". Lions live with, breed, and produce lions. Tigers, tigers. Monkeys, monkeys. Gorillas, gorillas, etc., ALL "after its own kind" even though they are of the same plant, fish, bird, animal, etc., kingdom or species classifications. God even COMMANDED Moses to NOT interbreed his livestock or sow his field with mixed seed (Lev. 19:19). Such NON-intermixing is God's "law" of His creations; or as some say, "the laws of nature". Therefore Biblically as well as logically it stands to reason that the SAME law was applied to man from the point where God made us look and speak differently (like cardinals and blue jays, monkeys and gorillas, etc.), and separated us at the Tower of Babel incident. That point or incident of Genesis Chapter 11 when God made the different races of man occurred AFTER God made the different kinds of birds, fish, etc., of Genesis Chapter 1, but that same law applies to man also. To understand God's command here, simply consider birds, fish, insects, fruit, man, etc., as being generalized categories of God's creations on earth. But then there are "kinds" WITHIN each category. Cardinals, Blue Jays, and Sparrows are "kinds" of "birds", just like whites, blacks, Orientals, and Arabs are "kinds" of "man" since the Tower of Babel. Nowadays we simply use the word "race" instead of kind of man. But the race IS the "kind" of man and God COMMANDS for ALL kinds to reproduce after its own kind. That means us/man too. Man is NO EXCEPTION to God's commands and laws of ALL His creations of nature.

Besides the fact that the continuation of separation is supported by New Testament scriptures, consider the fact that Jesus Himself lived amongst all the separation that still existed at that time and never told us to start living in diversity. There are NO scriptures commanding us to START interliving and intermarrying. Physical proof of

God still wanting us to be SEPARATE races, languages and religions living in our own countries - lies in the fact that we are STILL physically and socially different around the world. If God intended for man to live as "one" once again as man claims we are to do, then God would have very simply made us all instantly speak the same language and all be the same race as He initially created us. But He has not. That's the bottom line physical and logical PROOF in a nutshell that God is AGAINST us living in diversity. God has MAINTAINED OUR DIFFERENCES for His reason and purpose.

If you believe interliving, intermarrying and producing mixed offspring is okay to do, then if EVERYONE was to interlive, intermarry and have mixed offspring, mankind will end up being of the same physical appearance (race) and speak the same language, and become as "one" once again. Now go back and RE-READ Gen. 11:6 and UNDERSTAND it was for THAT very reason (BEING "ONE") that God decided to PUNISH US by making us different and separated in the first place!

To live in such diversity is going against God's commands and purpose for us while here on earth. It is Satan who is pushing for such intermixing and a New World Order/"beast system"/one world government and universal religion, and globalization in his attempt to bring us all back as "one" to SIN against God and accept the mark of the beast (Rev. 13:11-18). The U.S. government and any government that allows the immigration (legal or illegal) of people of any race, language, and/or religion differing from, or contrary to the established majority of the country and then forces its majority citizens to accept and cater to those minorities, is a government NOT pleasing to God and God will PUNISH those countries. The reason we are having so many problems here in the U.S. and abroad is because we as a people have ALLOWED our governments and countries as a whole to turn their backs on God.

Have you ever paid attention to the fact that almost all non-Caucasian non-Christian emigrants and refugees have gone and still go to countries that are (or were) mostly Christian and Caucasian? Why is that? It's because Satan is always attacking Christians, and Caucasians have been and are very easy to deceive into allowing such non-assimilating people into their countries and governments. Such non-assimilation of differing races, religions, languages and cultures will ALWAYS cause problems in ANY country that allows it. That's plain common sense logic as well.

Have we U.S. citizens allowed the U.S. to become the sinful Babylon prophesized about in the book of Revelation? We are told end-time Babylon has deceived "all the races (ethnos)" (Rev. 18:23). The prophesy then states that Babylon: "is fallen, is fallen" (Rev. 14:8 & 18:2) due to an act of "violence" (Rev. 18:21). It's quite odd to say the words: "is fallen, is fallen" TWICE. Could the 2 fallings the Apostle John saw be the Twin Towers collapsing during the 9-11 attacks in the most influential city and most influential country in the world? The Twin Towers collapsed at 9:59am and 10:28am respectively. That fits the: "in one hour" of verse 18:19. And could the "woman" in Chapter 17 who represents: "that great city which reigns over the kings of the earth" (Rev. 17:18) be the Statue of Liberty? Keep in mind that the headquarters of the United Nations, which "reigns over the kings of the earth", is there in New York City too. New York City may also be the most diverse city in the world. At any rate, God COMMANDS US to leave or "COME OUT" of Babylon (Rev. 18:4; Is. 48:20; and Jer. 51:6. LDS read D&C 133:7, etc.).

The Bible contains amazing prophesies concerning the intermixing of the races that no one seems to pay any attention to. ALL Bible prophesies MUST COME TRUE, or the Bible is a lie! Daniel 2:24-45 deals with Daniel interpreting the King's dream about the image figure as being various "kingdoms", which we nowadays refer to as empires, that were in power from that time period up until: "what will be in the latter days" (verse 28), which most scholars believe is occurring now. Verse 43 says: "As you saw iron mixed (intermix) with ceramic clay, they will mingle with (intermix) the seed of men, but they will not adhere to one another, just as iron does not mix (intermix) with clay." This prophesy clearly says the intermixing of the different races ("seed of men") during these last days before Jesus' return will not work out at all. Daniel foretold that "They" (men and their governments who have been deceived and corrupted by Satan and his demons) would intermix the races (get the different races to start interliving, intermarrying, and having mixed offspring), but this intermixing "WILL NOT ADHERE" (does NOT work out). There WAS a separation of the races, etc., back in those days. This big push for intermixing the races is a "latter days" occurrence after Jesus ascended, but it's not the first time intermixing occurred. Genesis 6:1-4 tells us the "sons of God" (the fallen angels) married the "daughters of men" (human women) and "bore children" that were a new race of "giants" (Nephilim). So the first account of intermixing occurred between the fallen angels and humans prior to God creating the different races. What did God do about that intermixing? He deliberately killed all the humans except for Noah (& his wife, their 3 sons & their wives) by flooding the earth (Gen. 6:5-8:22). Why did God spare Noah? Because Noah was a good man and "perfect in his generations" (Gen 6:9). In other words, Noah's genealogy and DNA had not been intermixed with the fallen angels or genetically corrupted in any way, so God spared Noah to replenish the earth with genetically pure humans as He initially created. Now fast forward to Luke 17:26-27 when Jesus foretold that before His return, things will be like the days of Noah with marrying and being given in marriage. That is a direct reference to the intermixed marriages of Gen. 6:1-4, only this time it's amongst the genetically different races that God created at the Tower of Babel. This parallels the intermixing of Dan. 2:43 and proves God is fully against ANY genetic intermixing amongst man that He created. In the interim of intermixing to the point of all becoming "one" race as Satan wants as previously pointed out, by intermixing our DNA we in essence are creating new races beyond what God created at the Tower of Babel – just like the fallen angels (Satan and his demons) created a new race in the days of Noah. It's Satan's goal to unpurify God's creations ANY WAY he can; directly as in the days of Noah, and indirectly now in these latter days. Will God punish us again now? If so, what are we to do, and what will Jesus do upon His return?

Isaiah 13:11-14 forewarns us that God: "will punish the world" to the point that: "EVERY MAN WILL TURN TO HIS OWN PEOPLE (RACE) and EVERYONE WILL FLEE TO HIS OWN LAND." (See also Jer. 51:9. LDS see 2Ne. 23:14).

Knowing these prophesy truths will occur is why Jesus told us that amongst the signs of the end of time: "RACE (ethnos) WILL RISE AGAINST RACE (ethnos)". (See Mth. 24:7; Mark 13:8; and Luke 21:10)

God also addresses the religion aspect by instructing us: "Do not be unequally yoked together with unbelievers...what communion has light with darkness...has a believer with an unbeliever?...Therefore COME OUT FROM AMONG THEM and BE SEPARATE says the Lord" (2 Cor. 6:14-17). Those of us who obey God's commands to "be separate" by forming new countries now, will also be fulfilling prophesy for those who didn't believe and participate now - to be able to "flee" to us before Jesus returns.

But the astonishing proof that God knew living in diversity would occur and that He wants us to be separate while here on earth in our earthly bodies, lies in the fact that when Jesus returns to set up His Millennial Kingdom for those of us who are alive then, He Himself will be separating us there too! Jesus said that when He returns in all His glory: "ALL THE RACES (ethnos) will be gathered before Him and HE WILL SEPARATE THEM one from another" (Mth. 25:31-32).

It doesn't get any more clear than these prophesies and commands of God. God knew Satan would deceive us to sin against God by living in diversity, and the Bible tells us how we can avoid His wrath and mark of the beast.

"Good borders make good neighbors".

Separation is a SOLUTION to end racial and religious tensions and make it easier for us to have LOVE for one another worldwide.

Let us Christians have the courage to honor and obey God, and let others either also believe these scriptures or use common sense logic to recognize that it's time for us all to "come out" of and "be separate" from "sinful Babylon" and countries having racial and religious tensions, and live with our "own people" of the same race, language and religion, in our "own land(s)" and "own country" (Jer. 51:9) by forming New Eden and other new countries now for the

sake of peace and love. (Read the Form New Countries and
New Eden links for
details).

Peace be with us.

Amen.

NOTE: This article and the formation of new countries
are based solely on God's commands and will for us here in
the earthly PHYSICAL realm. There is a clear difference
between what we are commanded to do in the physical
realm as opposed to the SPIRITUAL realm. Spiritually we
Christians are ALL "one in unity with Christ", and are all
members of one spiritual Church. Neither race nor
language is a factor for us spiritually. Worldwide, ALL
races are EQUALLY SAVED through Jesus. And
spiritually we Christians are ALL brothers and sisters in
Christ.

For thousands of years, new countries and governments have been formed through acts of violence and loss of many lives, including for the United States. But now in this age of modern technology we can effect peaceful formations through well-organized simultaneous movements this website is starting and sponsoring so we and our children can have better and safer futures. We can now petition our governments with proposals for fair distributions of land and resources for those wishing to form appropriate practicable new countries, plus ask the United Nations and other countries and individuals around the world for their political and physical support.

For example, here in the U.S. we currently have a fractured melting pot of races, religions, languages and cultures, yet also a lot of land and resources that can be proportionately divided between those who wish to separate amongst themselves. U.S. citizens have a CONSTITUTIONAL RIGHT: "of the people peaceably to assemble, and to petition the Government for a redress of grievances." The U.S. Declaration of Independence

bestows upon: "ALL men" the: "unalienable Rights" of:
"Life, Liberty, and the Pursuit of Happiness", and that:
"whenever any Form of Government becomes destructive
of" those Rights: "it is the Right of the People to alter or
ABOLISH IT, and to INSTITUTE NEW
GOVERNMENT." (See the 1st Amendment and
Declaration of Independence link, plus the ADAM
Government System link). Therefore it's considered a
RIGHT in the U.S. for us to petition the government with
our grievances of racial and religious tensions and
conflicts, and ask for redress of land and resources. Since
individual States (except perhaps Texas) are not permitted
to formally secede from the U.S., we must ask for land
areas - which may of course encompass a State or States in
whole or in part. Should the U.S. government refuse us
such pursuits of life, liberty and happiness, we then have
the Right to abolish the U.S. government and institute a
new government such as ADAM, where we can then divide
the land and resources fairly amongst ourselves. But
considering our U.S. Founding Fathers actually went to war
and basically stole the land and resources away from
Mother England and the Indians, and the U.S. government
is now completely comprised of people who are only

supposed to be fully representing us citizens, we should have no problem having our rightful peaceful petitions granted.

So as you can see, the U.S. system is quite unique and makes it very plausible and viable to start-up new countries using U.S. land. That's why it's important we start the movements here in the U.S. and lead by example.

Something we can put in our grievance proposals to be fair to the U.S. government is a default clause that would guarantee the allotted land would be given back if the new country fails to succeed. Once viable new country proposals using U.S. land have been established via this site, petitions for each will be placed onto the change.org site by the Main Office or its designees for the White House to address - as one means of petitioning under the U.S. Constitution.

In addition to all the problems that come with the racial and religious tensions, other grievances we can also cite in our petitions as reasons to be able to form new countries and governments - are our suffering from: constant involvement in wars and the threat of wars; living in fear of terrorist attacks; mass shootings and bombings at schools and other places; bomb threats; nuclear EMP (Electro-Magnetic Pulse) strikes; violence and bullying in our schools; violent gangs running amok; high crime rates; drug addicts and abusers; almost half the citizens receiving or seeking government handouts; government bailouts to large corporations; corruption within the government; corruption within large corporations; a government that caters to big business and big money lobbyists rather than to the best interests of its citizens; a public education system that has intentionally lowered its standards and dumbed down our children just to accommodate those who fail to keep up with a properly high level of education; government shutdowns due to bickering between divisive political party lines; the huge debt crisis; poor economy; homeless people; the huge disparity between the poor and elite wealthy; corrupt police, judges, prosecutors, and prison officials; unarmed or incapacitated suspects being shot and killed by police; police being ambushed and murdered; law enforcement being told not to do "racial profiling" even though profiling is absolutely necessary when it falls under "modus operandi"; illegal immigrants; a government system comprised of multiple political parties that has always caused division and arguments between the parties; citizens themselves being divided by inappropriate loyalties to pretentious political parties; career politicians and their bureaucracies and lies; theatrical mud-slinging campaigns every few years; excessive violence, sex, homosexuality and immorality played on public TV and radio for us and our children to be demoralized and degenerized by; no longer having the Bible taught in our U.S. public education system; Christian leaders and churches with agendas that are more concerned about self-promotion, expansion, and non-Biblical church functions rather than giving physical help to the needy as churches are supposed to; seeing our Rights, privacy and freedoms being constantly diminished; a government that refuses to mandate for a rapid changeover from fossil burning fuels to new clean air, environmental, cheap fuel technologies; a government that uses your tax dollars to give away many billions a year in free aid to other countries' governments and constantly meddles in other governments' affairs instead of tending to its own citizens' needs and problems at home; deteriorating infrastructures and power grids; are some prime examples. And with the tragic death of George

Floyd on 5/25/20, - the ensuing protests, riots and other criminal acts by left wing Democrats who seemingly want to overthrow the U.S. government, abolish it altogether, or at least rid it of all Republicans while wanting to live in racial and religious diversity, multiculturalism, open homosexuality and gender choosing (ALL of which the Democratic Party in general either fully endorses or does not oppose), perhaps now that Biden won, only Democrats should maintain and live in a "United States" with its current government system that would then only have their one political party. Republicans and everyone else who want no part of those ways would form their own countries with appropriate land and resources peacefully divided up amongst the U.S. and newly formed countries.

The U.S. is plenty big enough to divide up fairly. And all the different races, religions and languages here in the U.S. who propose their own countries being formed with U.S. land - will also be helping millions of people around the world who wish to live with their own people. Citizens of other countries can support our movements now and emigrate here to one of the newly forming countries of their people, or, be able to do so within their current countries because of the notoriety and success we'll be generating here in the U.S. Additionally, people anywhere in the world can become involved in the movement for a new country being formed anywhere else in the world by people of their race and religion and language. Whichever way, people around the world need to support all movements here in the U.S. and abroad so all fair and rightful proposals can succeed. THIS SITE will keep us ALL UNIFIED as the worldwide Central Headquarters for all involved.

Now is the time for whites, blacks, Hispanics, Arabs, Christians, Muslims, Jews, etc., to make proposals for our own new countries.

To give example and get things started, the Main Office hereby proposes forming a new country here in the U.S. for English-speaking Caucasian Christians who can be from the U.S. and other countries. The name proposed is New Eden. As for details and what land to petition the government to allot for New Eden, please read the New Eden link.

Simultaneously, Christians of other races and languages who wish to propose forming a new country for yourselves within the U.S. will also do so now using this site's links.

The same applies to people of other religions. U.S. blacks of the Nation of Islam also believe in establishing this movement for a peaceful separation into our own territories/land. For their details, go to www.finalcall.com and read "The Muslim Program" page of their "Wants" and "Beliefs". This site is your opportunity to form your own country and government NOW. There IS strength in numbers, and we all need to pool together in this Central Headquarters now so the U.S. government will take notice and comply.

Likewise with U.S. Mexicans who'd like to have their own country here. Use this site and support these overall movements, and ask Mexican citizens to join in. Ask the Mexican government for their support too.

Arabic Muslims can propose their own country and government.

The same with Hawaiians, American Indians, Asians, Jews, etc., who agree with this solution of peaceful separation and forming your own country and government, do so on this website's links.

"LGBT" (Lesbian, Gay, Bisexual, Transgendered) people can also propose forming their own country and government using this site.

The Main Office fully expects all Latter Day Saints/"Mormons" to give their immediate support and participation per their Articles of Faith numbers 10 and 12, 1Ne. 13:37, 3Ne. 21:1, Doctrines and Covenants 6:6, 11:6, 12:6, 14:6, 63:36, 64:38, 64:41-43, 105:32, 124:6, 136:18 & 31, etc. Now is the time for LDS to form their physical Zion utilizing this site and show they have faith that Joseph Smith was a prophet of God and that they truly believe in the writings in their Book of Mormon. Otherwise the Church of Jesus Christ of Latter Day Saints will lose credibility amongst its members as well as other denominations.

Additionally, people in countries all around the world should participate immediately and start making any proposals for other new countries via this site now. This includes especially SYRIAN REFUGEES and OTHER MIGRANTS in order to garner good support and respect from Europeans and other countries.

People, forming our new countries here and abroad is not only something we can take pride in, but also HAVE FUN doing in the process. There's so much to get excited about.

The names of each prospective new country must be established.

Requested land areas determined in coordination with other countries'
proposals.

Then each proposed country will need its own "Declaration of Independence" petition drawn up to formally request a secession with appropriate and fair land areas and resources. Through donations and any revenue generated on this site, an International law firm or firms will be hired by the Main Office, as well as any government lobbyists and representatives needed to speak on our behalves at the United Nations in order to accommodate the participants and supporters of these movements with the legal and other assistance necessary to help bring to fruition each prospective new country in the U.S. and around the world.

Constitutions will need to be written for each new country.

Flags designed and voted on. (See the New Eden link for its example).

National anthems composed and voted on.

Governments have to be installed with all its officials needing to be decided upon. New Eden and any or all new or current countries have the Main Office's consent to implement the copyrighted ADAM Government System outlined on this site. It's completely innovative and another must-read. (See the ADAM link). With ADAM, people can start campaigning NOW for King or Queen of their prospective country.

Participants can also propose any government system for any country now, and/or campaign to be its Leader.

So no matter if you use this site to propose a new country and/or new government system, and/or campaign to be King, Queen, President, or other leader, and/or partake in chatting and voting on these important historical matters, or just quietly read what others are saying; the Main Office wants that EVERYONE ENJOY THEMSELVES.

Regardless of our racial, religious and other differences, we MUST now ALL focus on and support this COMMON GOAL of PEACEFUL separation movements. We very simply start with EVERYONE using ONLY this site and its links.

ALL MOVEMENTS, especially for forming new countries using U.S. land, NEED to be organized on this Central Headquarters site so they can all be coordinated properly with accurate proposals of land for each new country. We all need a Central Headquarters to maintain organization for participants and supporters and KEEP these movements well coordinated, and this site is it.

The Main Office hereby extends its copyright claim for these movements to form new countries and governments, to all participants and supporters who utilize this site.

Get involved and take pride in your Central Headquarters and its exciting, unique movements.

Worldwide, people will see how the links allow anyone to create their own profiles and country and government proposals. As interest and participation increases, this site can expand accordingly with customized links to more specifically accommodate the different races, religions, languages, and proposed countries.

Although this site and its links are all free to use, donations are greatly needed as you can imagine due to the magnitude of expenses for all that's involved in getting these movements started and maintained, and the law firm(s) and any representatives hired. The formula for success for everyone, is for Central Headquarters to grow in direct proportion with the totality of these joint movements being birthed. We need participants and moral supporters of all movements to please give whatever physical support you can; especially through financial donations on this site (See Donations link), of WHATEVER amount you can afford however often - so we have a CYCLE OF SUPPORT from us individuals of Central Headquarters through to the overall movements formed and all the way to success for all fair and rightful new country formations WORLDWIDE; which of course means success for all us individuals who get involved in this Central Headquarters in the first place.

So please join in now.

BE A PART OF WORLD HISTORY IN THE MAKING!

Let's make our children proud, happy and safe.

We CAN do it people.

WELCOME

TO THE OFFICIAL WEBSITE FOR

For an Able government, raise
Cain this Eve for ADAM

The ADAM Government System is a completely innovative form of government proposed for implementation in New Eden and any new country being created or already in existence. ADAM is an acronym for: A Democratic Absolute Monarchy.

Throughout the world there are different forms of monarchies - such as Constitutional, Traditional, Absolute, Parliamentary, Modified, and Hereditary. The key word in ADAM is "Democratic" because its purpose is to be a true democracy where the majority of citizens ultimately rule the country through direct voting. The U.S. and other countries that claim to be democracies are in actuality "Republic" forms of government. (See the U.S. Constitution and Pledge of Allegiance). With ADAM, the King or Queen would only be an "Absolute Monarch" in that he or she would have the authority to put the votes, laws, and actions into immediate effect without any bureaucratic red tape delays. There would not be any Congress (Senate or House of Representatives) or Parliament to slow things down or play "politics as usual" with voting along party lines. The people will represent themselves through direct votings by eligible voters. Which citizens qualify as "eligible voters" would be determined by each countries' Constitutions.

This is the 21st century. We no longer need lying pompous arrogant career politicians to allegedly "represent" us when we can represent ourselves now, including from the comfort of our own homes. In the U.S. and other modernized countries, modern technologies would be used to cast votes for people's convenience and rapid tallying. The Monarch would enact the will of the majority people. Each country's citizens would determine within their constitutions - what percentage the majority vote needs to be for elections.

The Monarch would also have expert advisors in all areas necessary to run a country at its most efficient. If problems arise, the Monarch can get recommendations from the advisors. When multiple feasible solution recommendations exist, the Monarch would present them to the people to vote on, just as with any new laws proposed.

To put the ADAM structure into an analogy people should be able to relate to; - think of how stereotypical non-denominational Christian community churches and/or some Baptist and other denominations of Churches are structured. You have the Church itself overall, its Pastor, Associate Pastors, and the Church members. The Church = the country or government. The Pastor = the Monarch. The Associate Pastors = the expert advisors. And the members = the citizens. The Church members get to vote in a Pastor and oust him even though he's their "leader". The Pastor can select Associates, but the members can oust Associates or instruct the Pastor to make replacements. Although the Pastor is the leader of the Church, he must always please the majority of its eligible voting members or face being ousted. The same applies under ADAM. The Monarch is the leader of the country. He or she appoints advisors, makes decisions and takes actions, but is always subject to the will of the majority citizen voters who have the ultimate final say-so.

So long as the Monarch is doing a good job, he or she can remain in power until death or stepping aside to exercise the option for one of his or her children to be the successor. But if the people feel the Monarch isn't doing a good job, he or she can be ousted and replaced by whoever the majority elect. The same applies if a good Monarch dies or wishes to step down or "retire" and the people don't want an offspring to automatically replace him or her. The child or one of the advisors can be interim Monarch while people wishing to be the new Monarch would campaign and an election would take place. Such specifics would need to be outlined in each country's constitution at the onset.

Meanwhile, any existing or prospective country's citizens wishing to install ADAM now - can get started NOW via this site. Interested persons will campaign using this site's links, and the country's citizens or prospective citizens will vote for their Monarch. This is how each country will establish its very 1st Monarch under ADAM, - by holding democratic elections to vote for campaigners. And installing ADAM eliminates the strong divisiveness caused by having multiple political parties under other forms of government.

If you've ever said to yourself: "If only I were King (or Queen)", then NOW is YOUR opportunity to try and make your dream come true. Read the "HOW TO" link for details. Even if you don't succeed, you should have a lot of fun trying. Non-campaigners will also enjoy reading what the campaigners have to say, and can chat with them on the appropriate link of this site.

Everyone enjoy yourselves, and long live the King or Queen.

NEW EDEN FLAG

New Eden is the name of the new country the Main Office has proposed being formed for English speaking Caucasian Christians, using land and resources provided by the U.S. government.

The proposed flag design is on the preceding page. The cross represents Jesus and symbolizes New Eden is a Christian nation. The white background symbolizes New Eden is comprised of Caucasians ("whites"). That allows for Christians of other races who also form new countries - to use the same design with a different background color to symbolize their race. The color of the cross (& border) is "royal" purple to symbolize Jesus as King of kings, especially since the innovative ADAM Government System of having a Monarch is proposed for New Eden. The red and blue rays emitting from the cross symbolize the blood and water Jesus shed while being crucified for the salvation of all who believe in Him.

As for what land area(s) to ask the U.S. government for, that will depend largely on how many people give their support and truly desire and commit to becoming citizens of New Eden NOW. If only a few hundred thousand to a few million are interested and involved, perhaps one of the less populated Hawaiian Islands such as Kauai or Hawaii, plus an Alaskan island can be requested to have variety. If many millions join in now, then perhaps the land areas of Idaho, Wyoming, Montana, Utah, Oregon, Washington, and a small Hawaiian and/or other island in the South Pacific or off the coast of southern California. Asking for a Hawaiian island also opens the door for native Hawaiians to petition to form their own country with the remaining islands (except maybe Oahu since the U.S. would likely want to keep Oahu because of the military base there. If so, New Eden and the Hawaiian country could have agreements with the U.S. to let the U.S. maintain defending them while they get properly established).

It's best New Eden not be landlocked in order to maintain its autonomy and all around independence more effectively and efficiently.

Although New Eden is for Christian Caucasians, it will be an impossibility initially for ALL citizens to be 100%

"white" due to all the intermixing that's been going on. What's important is for all citizens to be committed to New Eden being a 100% English-speaking Christian nation for Caucasians. Having SINCERE God-loving God-fearing Spirit-filled Christian citizens striving to be a nation pleasing to God is a key for New Eden to succeed too.

Old and New Testament Bible scriptures foretell of a new wicked Babylon (possibly the U.S.) that God's people ("Zion") will be living in, plus the coming of the mark of the beast. It's imperative for Christians to keep in mind that ALL who receive the mark of the beast SHALL be KILLED by Jesus, TORMENTED by fire and brimstone, and have NO REST day or night. (See Rev. 13:16-18, 14:9-11 & 19:20-21). The only way to avoid the wrath of God and the beast and his mark, is to form new Christian nations (for New Eden and other races & languages) pleasing to God. All Christians are commanded to do so as the physical Zion descendants of the Israelites and entire body of Believers. God commands: "Up Zion! Escape, you who dwell with the daughter of Babylon" (Zechariah 2:7). "Forsake her and let us go EVERYONE TO HIS OWN COUNTRY" (Jer. 51:9). See the Living in Diversity link for many other scriptures. Caucasian American Christians AND all supporters and participants can start the movement for New Eden now by using this site's links.

If you haven't already read the previous 4 links, please do so for many details.

For those of you who want to install ADAM and campaign to be King or Queen of New Eden, or if you wish to propose a different government system people can vote on, and/or to read more innovative ideas for New Eden (and other new countries), please proceed and read the "HOW TO" link for details.

In this age of modern technology, we CAN garner rapid support and accomplish our goal of forming New Eden (and other new countries) and implementing the changes we want and need - in peaceful manners.

The time to act is NOW - for the sake of peace and our children's futures.

Let's roll.

Victory thru Jesus - Glory to God!

HOW TO: Propose New Countries &/or Government Systems &/or
Campaign to be a King, Queen, President, or other Leader

Greetings to all. If you've read this site's links in order, you've already seen the proposals for the New Eden country/kingdom and ADAM Government System. If not, please read them to give yourself ideas and examples for proposing your new country and/or government system. Once you've formulated your ideas for either or both, click onto the appropriate "Propose" link. You will find further instructions there to assist you in setting up your free profile.

Similarly, if you wish to campaign to be King, Queen, President or other leader of a newly proposed government for a current or newly proposed country, first read the remainder of this link in its entirety, then click onto the appropriate "Campaign" link and read the instructions there to set up your free profile.

Following is a very thorough example that's sure to give you many ideas, and its format should be replicated by all campaigners to make it easiest and best for all readers to compare everyone, ask their questions, and make their decisions:

Hello people. My name is Bobby Fratta and I am an English speaking Christian Caucasian campaigning to be the 1st King of New Eden under the ADAM Government System. I first should explain that I am also the author, copyright holder and claimant of all the articles and concepts on this site. I've designated and instructed for this site to be Central Headquarters for all you participants and supporters because I'm unfortunately also incarcerated on Texas' infamous Death Row and have no access to a computer or the internet. But thankfully I'm blessed with people out there setting things up and helping me try to fulfill my dream to help us end racial and religious tensions by forming new countries; especially New Eden - where I want my children and grandchildren to live. It truly is my heart's desire to help others even though I'm imprisoned, and I hope to see my dream fulfilled. I'm 100% dedicated to the success of this endeavor for all involved and all the way through to each new country being formed and/or new government systems installed in the U.S. and abroad, and vow to do all I can from in here. Yes, I dream big. But I'm also an honest person and a realist. That's why I'm setting things up for once enough donations are made, an International law firm can be retained to handle legal, business and financial matters for even if I should die. I want to make sure this site and all you individuals and ensuing movements will be able to carry on to succeed without me regardless if I spend the rest of my life in prison, get acquitted and released, or die. I'm not necessary for you all and this, your Central Headquarters to continue forward to success with the movements. But you all are! You can make my dream come true for yourselves and loved ones, and for my children and grandchildren even if I'm gone. I hope you'll please do so.

To tell you more about myself, I was born February 22nd (coincidentally our 1st President, George Washington's birthday) in 1957 on Long Island, New York, and lived there until I was 21. I was raised Catholic and became a "born again Christian" shortly after my dad died when I was just 17. I worked my way from 11th grade through community college, graduated with an A.A.

Degree, then got hired by a major airline and moved to Hartford, then Las Vegas, then Houston in 1980. I got married in 1983 and have 3 children I love with all my heart, unconditionally. I loved being a family man and "Mr. Mom" soccer dad. Raising and nurturing my children was my happiness. I had quit the airlines to become a firefighter, emergency care attendant, and police officer for 10 years up until 1994. It was then I got accused of capital murder, arrested 5½ months later, convicted in 1996 and sentenced to be executed. I've proclaimed my innocence from the onset and have asked every branch of our government to investigate my case, civil rights violations and other claims, and turn over all the evidence the police and prosecutors have been withholding so I can prove I've been framed. But ALL the branches have refused and ignored my pleas for help and justice.

When I was arrested in 1995 it was a blessing in disguise in that it was an opportunity for me to be able to read all the books of the Bible for the first time, and truly fellowship with God. I desire and strive to make Jesus Lord of my life, and feel inspired to do and reveal God's will for us. My eyes have been opened to all the deception I've always accepted as being truths and normal. I see now how deviously Satan deceives us and how ignorant we Christians are to God's truths because we fail to READ the Bible. I want to encourage ALL Christians to read and study the entire Bible for themselves and become educated to God's own inspired words and truths.

In 2000 I started receiving what I can only call revelations through the Holy Spirit to write about the formation of a new government system and countries. I had never experienced anything like that before, felt very awkward about it, and kept trying to stop the entire undertaking. Yet I felt "guided" to continue.

Because I'm a victim of government corruption, I vow to fight to end it if elected King. I would be a devoted King and strive to make New Eden a nation pleasing to God. I love and fear God. I proclaim Jesus Christ as the only begotten Son of God the Father, my Lord and Savior, and the true King of kings.

I want to serve God and my brothers and sisters in Christ or "the people".

I am a logical person now and not sold by emotions like most people seem to be nowadays.

I want to make New Eden the safest, friendliest, most desirable country to live in.

For those who wish to believe I am not innocent and therefore don't deserve your support, please don't let your emotions stop you from supporting these movements. And along the lines of logic and God's word, I point out that Moses murdered an Egyptian (see Exodus 2:11-12), yet God exalted him to work miracles and lead God's initial chosen people (the Israelites) to the promised land. King David committed adultery with Bathsheba, then intentionally sent her husband Uriah into frontline battle so he'd be killed (2 Sam. 11:1-17), yet God exalted him and called David a man after God's own heart (Acts 13:22). And the Apostle Paul who wrote approximately half the books of the New Testament, persecuted the early Christians, approved and oversaw the murder of Stephen (Acts 7:54-8:3), yet he was still hand-picked by Jesus to be an Apostle (Acts 9:1-6 & 10:9). So as you can see, innocence does NOT even matter to God. God exalts murderers too because He knows and cares about what's in a man's heart as priority. God knows my heart already, so all I can do for you readers is reveal it to you via this site. But because I don't expect anyone to believe I'm innocent, I'm fighting to prove it. (See all my Pro Se filings in the courts for MANY unreported details, or simply read: www.robertfratta.com and/or https://bobbyfratta.wixsite.com/homepage for some of my important and current filings).

If you're tired of all the campaigns and broken promises from career politicians, and promises that take far too long to get put into effect; if you want to do away with the corruption and politics as usual in government; if you're tired of seeing countries turn their backs on God and desire to form a Christian country pleasing to Him (plus other countries), then please support me in this endeavor.

Perhaps God has chosen me for this endeavor because He knows the U.S. government took my children away from me, prevented me from raising them and being there to help my mom and be there for her when she died, falsely convicted me, is trying hard to murder me, and has refused to investigate my claims, thus denying me of several Constitutional Rights and my "unalienable Rights to Life, Liberty, and the Pursuit of Happiness", whereby giving ME SPECIFICALLY the Right to seek redress of my grievances by authority of the 1st Amendment as well as seeking the formation of a new government in accordance with the Declaration of Independence - moreso than most other U.S. citizens.

If the U.S. government refuses to let us form New Eden and other countries with U.S. land and we vote to abolish the government and install ADAM, then please elect me King of the U.S. I would firstly pardon myself, of course, then convene with the leaders of other movements of this Central Headquarters and fairly divide the land and resources amongst us so we can then form New Eden and other new countries.

MY PHILOSOPHIES:
First of all, it is my belief based on the Bible, that we should elect a KING; not a Queen. 1 Peter 2:17 commands us to: "Honor THE KING". Other scriptures that support

women not be placed into positions of authority over men are: Deut. 17:14-15; 1 Sam. 10:22-25 & 16:1-3; Hosea 1:11 & 3:4-5; Isaiah 3:12; 1 Cor. 11:3-9 & 14:34-35; Eph. 5:22-24; Col. 3:18; 1 Tim. 2:11-12 & 3:12; Titus 2:4-5; and 1 Pet. 3:1-6. (LDS also see Mosiah 29:13, and A. of F. #12). I firmly believe the Bible to be the inspired word of God (2 Tim. 3:16). For any women or men who disagree, that's between you and God. Pray about it, and please don't consider me to be any kind of misogynist just because I take the Bible literally and seriously. I believe we all should, and I ask women to please support me in this endeavor also. I greatly need and appreciate women.

If I were elected King, I would immediately decree New Eden a Christian nation, put the teaching of the Bible back into our schools and public education system, declare the 7th day (Saturday) as the Sabbath, and God's Holy Days as our holidays (See Leviticus Chapter 23). I would expose any past or present lies, cover-ups and conspiracies made known to me; including such things as whether we really landed on the moon, UFOs and any alien life forms, the JFK assassination, and especially if we already have cures for any diseases and clean, cheap substitutes for fossil fuels. I would make any cures and substitutes available quickly. I would strive to form and maintain an incorruptible government that New Eden citizens can look up to and be proud of.

Following is a summary outline of my philosophies:

I AM FOR:
* Striving to obey God's commands of us, yet maintaining a true separation of Church and State functions, obligations and duties as Jesus noted (Mth. 22:21).
* Increased individual freedoms and rights to privacy.
* Focused on being the most technologically advanced nation in the world in everything from military weapons and defense, to crime fighting, education, and the medical field.
* Doing what's in the best interest for the majority and country as a whole.
* Protecting citizens from others, but not from themselves.
* Promoting family values and morals and having them taught in the public education system.

* Providing a new high standard, high quality, high technology education system which ensures an equal education to all public schools and students.

* Equal justice for all citizens.

* Flat tax rates. Probably a consumption tax on products and services.

* Encouraging "the church" to take care of needy citizens.

* Hiring the best minds and most qualified people for government jobs.

* A government funded community in one location for those needy citizens the church, their families, friends, and private organizations can't or won't take care of.

* Having one set of federal laws that apply to all citizens. (No more separate State laws).

* Improving and preserving our environment as necessity dictates for the citizens.

* Rapid development and implementation of practical power sources and engines which do not burn fossil fuels and are pollution free.

* Complete truth in advertising.

* A government's function and subsequent usage of tax dollars being for infrastructure provisions and

maintenance, education, research and development, and the overall protection of its citizens and borders.

* Causing citizens to depend upon the government rather than God, "the church", their families, friends, and/or themselves.

* Meddling in other countries' affairs.

* Welfare, Social Security, food stamps, etc.

* Government involvement in marriages and divorce. (Unless of course laws are broken or civil suits have to be filed).

* Free government aid to other countries.

* A New World Order or One World Government and globalization.

* Affirmative action and telling citizens who they must hire and promote.

* Having any labor unions.

* Forced integration.

* Big government and politics as usual.

* Lobbying and special interest groups, and any government officials accepting any money, item, or favor.

* Excessive violence, sex, homosexuality, vulgarity, or lewd and immoral behavior aired on free public access sources (See Family Values/Moral Standards for details).

* Recognizing corporations as an individual for taxes.

* Any branch of government placing women into positions of authority over men, per the Bible. (See scriptural references under My Philosophies). Individuals in private businesses may of course do as they wish.

MY STANCES:

Following are my basic stances on some major issues. But these would change based on what's best for the country and whether the majority people want alternative courses of action from me. As you read these, keep in mind that the current U.S. Constitution would not apply at all since we would write a completely new Constitution for New Eden under the ADAM Government System.

My stances are in no particular order of importance.

CRIME:

I'm hard on crime, but I also strongly believe in a person's sincere repentance and rehabilitation since we all sin and fall short of the glory of God (Rom. 3:23).

I would immediately strive to have a Truth Telling Technology ("3T") developed which when administered to a person, that person is unable to lie and can only tell the truth and reveal all details. Then anyone who is suspected of a crime must submit to having the 3T administered - which will immediately prove innocence or guilt in detail. No criminal trials will be needed, but all 3T applications will be videotaped for integrity purposes.

I want set punishments for every crime, with punishments greater for repeat offenders. The set punishments will apply to everyone equally. No leniencies for celebrities, the wealthy, or government officials and employees.

After the punishment phase, the 3T will again be administered to determine whether the person is still a threat to society. A violent person will not be released from prison until he is determined to no longer be a threat to society by his own testimony under the 3T. This is to prevent repeat offenders from being an occurrence. The 3T would also be applied to anyone out on any probation phase in lieu of using probation officers to judge how the person is doing.

The 3T will be a tremendous deterrent to all forms of crime and can also be used in civil suits to resolve all "he said/she said" situations.

As an example of its effectiveness, let's say we need to get rid of a violent gang. We simply catch one gang member and administer the 3T. He then gives us the names and whereabouts of other gang members he knows. So we bring them in and apply the 3T. They give us more names, and so on, until all the members and leader are apprehended. All possibly in one day's work.

The 3T will be used to deter and capture any corrupt police officers, prison officials, government officials, spies, etc. No one will be above the laws established for New Eden. But keep in mind there will be a lot less laws than the U.S. has because there won't be any separate State laws, and the rights, privacies and freedoms of New Eden citizens will be increased.

With the 3T in use, any prosecutors and criminal court judges can be phased out and save tax payer dollars.

To further battle crime, high dollar rewards will be a standing offer to citizens who report such things as unsolved crimes, plans to commit crimes, people in possession of unregistered guns and illegal weapons, etc. And citizens who report such criminal activity would not be called "whistleblowers". Instead we would come up with a more commendable and honorable title such as "Morals Hero" for their care and courage.

Parents would be held accountable and liable for their children's actions who are too young to be punished by the government.

"Problem children" must be reported to the government. The government will pay for evaluation and treatment of uninsured problem children. If we tend to our problem children while they are young, we are helping them and ourselves for when they become adults within society.

"Mentally unstable adults" must also be reported and tended to.

Pet owners would be held liable for their pets. No aggressive or dangerous breeds of animals, such as Pit Bull dogs, will be allowed as pets in New Eden.

As for whether or not we have a Death Penalty for certain crimes, I have punishments in mind which people may prefer and would present them to the public if elected King. It's up to the voters to determine what ultimate punishment they want in effect, and I would implement it.

PUBLIC EDUCATION SYSTEM:
I would raise, equalize and standardize the quality of education in all public schools via a high technology Public Education System ("PES") of teaching that would be implemented in lieu of trying to raise and standardize the quality of teachers themselves. A teacher's role will be more of an organizer and monitor since things like computer videos and virtual reality devices would be used for the majority of teaching and learning. Teachers would

also watch for and report mentally unstable, aggressive, bully, problem, and violent students in order to make our schools safer.

The Bible, morals, family values, the laws, and crime and punishments are subjects that will be taught. Sex or safe sex courses can be taught at a certain age too, but it can be voted on along with other issues.

The new PES would be designed for our children to do more work at school rather than at home. In other words, less homework.

Because the PES would involve using a standardized high-tech means of teaching, parents can also use the system for home schooling.

There would be no forced integration between school districts, nor would it be necessary in any way due to the equality of the PES.

After school sports will not be part of the PES, and I would not use government tax dollars to fund after school sports. Such sports do nothing to help advance a nation or sustain it in a crisis, and is not part of school education. I feel way too much emphasis is placed on such sports and one of the reasons our society has been dumbed down. Education should stimulate the brain, not the brawn. But I am for exercising for health during schooling hours, and believe in keeping gym classes structured for such beneficial exercising.

CIVIL RIGHTS:

As I stated previously, an entirely new Constitution will be drawn up, which can include a Bill of Rights or Law of Rights.

The government's duty should be to protect citizens from others, but not from themselves. Adults should have the right to do what they want to themselves IN PRIVACY, (i.e. - drugs, prostitution, suicide, assisted suicide). Such private and consensual actions amongst adults, should be between the individuals and GOD; not the government. Only when an individual's actions could or do adversely affect others physically, will it be illegal, (i.e. - getting drunk in privacy, but then driving in public).

Adults should not have to wear seatbelts or motorcycle or bicycle helmets. Insurance companies would probably charge higher premiums and/or deductibles; but that's between them and their customers to work out. Children WOULD have to be placed in car seats or seatbelts and wear helmets.

I would increase citizens' rights to privacy. Some examples are that no unauthorized biographies will be permitted, and no publicizing of sexually explicit photos, videos, or personal writings of others without their consent. Consent would be mandatory in various areas to protect the right of privacy.

There would be no affirmative action, discrimination, age or gender bias laws. The government should not tell citizens who they should or shouldn't hire or promote.

No labor unions will be permitted.

As for government jobs, the best qualified people will be hired; whomever that may be. It will be in the country's best interest and overall welfare and progress to hire the greatest minds in the world, including from other countries if necessary (as guest workers if of other races and religions) to make New Eden the most technologically advanced nation in the world. However, women will not be placed into positions of authority over men; only over other women. (See the scriptures cited under My Philosophies).

FAMILY VALUES/MORAL STANDARDS:
Family values and moral standards will be taught in the Public Education System along with the Bible.

Because we, and most especially our children, become demoralized and degenerized as products of our environment of what we routinely see, hear and read mostly via free and easily accessible means such as TV, radio, and the internet, I want to impose a law making it illegal to have excessive violence, sex, homosexuality, vulgarity, and lewd and immoral behavior aired and/or displayed on FREE public access sources. Such TV shows would have to be "pay per view" only. Such songs cannot be aired on the radio. Such websites or blogs must also be accessed by a fee and/or adult registration. All FREE public access sources would have to be more wholesome.

I'm also for either banning excessively violent video games, or having age
and/or other restrictions imposed. We can hold a vote to determine how to handle such video games.

TAXES:
I would impose flat tax rates. No write-offs. No deductions. No corporate or other exemptions. No incentives or breaks for marriage. Every individual would pay flat tax rates. I favor doing this by implementing a federal sales tax on all purchases made. Having a federal sales or consumption tax means all visitors would be paying it also, which would help in keeping the rate low. I would like for this federal tax to be the only tax imposed upon us. I don't want to have any State, city, county, school district, water district, or other separate taxes like the U.S. currently has. I want to see if we can make it work with having just the one tax on all products and services sold, bought, or consumed, and keep matters as simple as possible. I also favor having a federal lottery as a

supplement to help make this one tax work. It can also be modified by doing such things as imposing a higher flat tax rate on high priced products deemed as luxury items. But because I believe a government's function and tax dollar usage should only be for infrastructure, education, research and development, and protecting its citizens and borders, plus not being involved in all these wars, and greatly downsizing the government through implementation of the Truth Telling Technology (3T) and other means, government expenditures will be GREATLY REDUCED; meaning less tax dollars needed to run the government efficiently.

The 3T would also be used for tax evasion suspects and audits.

LOTTERY:
I would like to have a federal lottery to help keep the flat tax low.

MARRIAGE/DIVORCE:
The government would not be involved in marriages at all. Marriage will strictly be a function of "the church", along with granting divorces. Marriage is something done

between the couple and God; not the couple and government.

The government will of course become involved in any criminal or civil matters arising as a result of the church not being able to resolve a divorce. This would include child custody, property disputes, prenuptial agreement violations or contestings, and child endangerments. The 3T will be used in such civil matters where the government is needed. I would also encourage that prenuptial agreements be done before all marriages. Doing so gives couples the opportunity to really get to know each other, and avoids messy divorces.

There will be no marriage incentives or tax breaks, and no laws prohibiting polygamy or concubines since we will have increased freedoms and rights.

ABORTION:
In terms of being King in a democratic government (ADAM), I would enact whatever the majority decided on. But if left up to me, I would have no government funded abortions - unless it was a case of life threatening necessity

to save the life of an uninsured mother, which I hope would be extremely rare. In accordance with the government protecting citizens from one another but not from themselves, I would vaguely define a citizen as "one who can sustain his or her life on his or her own accord" in regards to a fetus/unborn child. Up to the point where a fetus can be delivered and survive on its own accord, it technically is still a part of the mother and therefore not under the government's obligation to protect it from the mother. It therefore should not be illegal to have or perform an abortion until the fetus can be considered a citizen. Such an action would be between the mother, abortionist, and God. But I would have laws regarding the ages of the mother and fetus, notification to the father - with his input (except if a rapist), notification to the parents of underage mothers and fathers - with their input, and advisements of alternatives prior to any abortion. I would hope that with the Bible, morals, etc., being taught in our Public Education System, unwanted pregnancies and abortions can become non-existent anyway. Additionally, something like the morning after pills can be sold over the counter to keep matters private between the woman, man, and God, and may be what rape victims would want and prefer.

It should be illegal for any PUBLIC displays of homosexuality, and the sin of homosexuality would be taught in our PES along with all sins in the Bible. But what homosexuals do IN PRIVATE is between them and God; not the government.

Being that the government would not be involved in any marriages, that ends
any debate on gay marriage from a government standpoint.

Individual citizens would be able to "discriminate" if they want - for who they hire and promote; meaning no one could tell them to hire or promote homosexuals if they don't want to.

Being that it's in the best interest for the government to hire the best qualified people for jobs, that would include homosexuals so long as they are not being openly flamboyant or flaunting their homosexuality. It's wrong for anyone to openly flaunt their sins. Even though God knows we all commit sins, He certainly would not be pleased by a government that employed people who flaunted their sins. Nor would hiring such people set a good example for our children. I don't anticipate such homosexuals even wanting to be citizens of New Eden.

MINIMUM WAGE:
I want capitalism and free market enterprise, but I would impose laws against fraud, false advertising, and swindling. As with any criminal act, the 3T would be applied to all suspected violators to keep businessmen honest.

I feel we should establish a fair minimum wage based on the economy, cost of living, and value of the dollar (or New Eden currency if it's in our best interest to have our own).

If necessary, I'd start New Eden off with opening up importation of select products (such as pharmaceuticals and motor vehicles) in order to keep prices and the cost of living down. I'd then regulate importation based on how our economy is doing (supply and demand, the job market, unemployment rate, trade agreements with other countries, etc.). Federal taxes must be paid on all imported products the same as any product or service purchased while in New Eden.

Although capitalism allows for any individual to become wealthy, it doesn't seem right that the U.S. has such disparity between the wealthy and the poor or lower income people. Many people seem troubled by this gap. I feel if New Eden were to start getting that way, we can hold an election to determine if the majority wants something done about it. If so, I believe we can come up with something unique that will still allow for people to attain wealth just as quickly, but then slow things down after a certain point to funnel money to others. I would publicize the plan(s) so people can vote to decide if something is implemented. I have a few ideas in mind already, but would also convene with my advisors for any other plan(s).

GUN CONTROL:
First we can hold a vote to determine if New Eden citizens wish to retain a right to bear arms. If so, I'm for having strict laws regarding the buying, selling, registering,

manufacturing safety standards, and what kind of arms private citizens can have.

As part of the registration process, a free safety course can be given, and background checks run. The 3T can be used here too, to make sure the person does not have any impending criminal intention(s). We can vote on this also.

Mentally unstable people will not be allowed to purchase or have any guns.

MILITARY DEFENSE:
I would initially ask the U.S. to maintain our defense while we get New Eden established. Then I'd immediately strive to have the most advanced technologies developed that will enable New Eden to have the most superior weapons defense system in the world for our protection, peace and freedom. I want to utilize high technologies rather than our troops as often as possible. With a system I have in mind, none of our military personnel would be placed in any front-line war combat zone risk. I also would not have any troops stationed around the world. I would use

our military mostly as homeland border patrol and National Guard.

I favor using our military as all our local law enforcement instead of all the law enforcement departments the U.S. has around the country. I believe it would be best to have just the one federal police department so everything is coordinated by the military. Such a military police department allows personnel the ability to transfer to other areas of New Eden, plus to other divisions within the military if they want. I feel having a military police department would immediately avoid the rampant corruption problems like the U.S. has in most of their local law enforcements, and gives us better protection all around while we work on getting the 3T implemented. It saves us on tax dollars too.

I want our military personnel to be multi-faceted, elite, professional, and well paid.

ENVIRONMENT:
I'd seek to replace fossil burning fuels with environmentally safe ones, and rapidly develop and

implement engines and other power sources that do not use fossil fuels and are pollution free and low cost to operate.

I would also have scientists working right away on means of less costly electricity production. Besides solar and wind, surely new and better technologies are out there or can be developed, including for usage by private citizens for their homes so they don't have to be dependent upon corporate utilities and power grids that get damaged and fail and leave people without power all too often.

I believe in having recycling of items such as paper, plastic, and metals, and having laws against air, water and land pollutions. If need be, I'd have more trees planted.

I'm for having and maintain parks.

FOREIGN RELATIONS/TRADE:
I would do my best to establish good relations with other nations. I believe it's alright to help other countries through trade agreements so long as New Eden benefits as well. But because the Bible tells us that it is God Himself who enlarges nations and destroys them (Job 12:23), I do

not believe in bailing out other countries' governments. I feel if a government fails, it's because it was not pleasing to God and therefore changes are needed.

I do not believe in New Eden becoming a member of the United Nations or any world organization if their functions are to unite the nations of the world together under one governing body or New World Order. I am also opposed to a World Criminal Court. I believe in establishing our own good relations with other countries autonomously.

Although I firmly believe in following Jesus' commission for us to go to other nations and preach the gospel and make disciples (Mark 16:15-16 and Mth. 28:19-20), we are to do that as individuals and/or through the church; NOT as a government. And notice the directives are to: "go to" other nations, not bring them to our country to live with us; and: "preach" the gospel, not give billions of dollars in free government aid or meddle in their affairs and fight their wars for them. I don't believe we should meddle in other countries' affairs because doing so is likely interfering with God's desire for each country to "grope for

Him and find Him" (Acts 17:26-27) and setting ourselves up for punishment even though we may want to think our meddling was for the good of humanity. God's priority for mankind is SALVATION, which is why we are told to preach the gospel rather than give free aid. I also believe it's wrong to allow refugees to come and interlive with us. I invite the Syrian (& other countries') refugees to utilize this site to propose forming their own new country, including within existing Syria. I believe their doing that would generate a lot of support and respect.

Many countries consider the U.S. a bully and meddler and we are under constant threat of attacks and have lost so much of our freedoms in the country labeled as the so-called "land of the free". New Zealanders don't get searched at their airports like we do in the U.S., and they have much more freedom than we do based on what I've read. So I want New Eden to be a peaceful nation unto itself, and not meddle. Yet I would have technology developed to protect us from any country and attack if ever necessary.

I would do what I believe is in accordance with God's will and in the best interest of New Eden when it comes to foreign relations and trade.

MEDIA SOURCES/THE PRESS:

"The Press" is to report "the News" as it occurred. Not its interpretations of that News. No media source or individuals employed or compensated in any capacity therein may give any News-related report that deviates from the actual facts of the event reported on. In other words, there won't be any more left or right slanted "freedom of the Press" to harbor agendas of intentionally influencing the public's opinion. Only facts and unedited quotes and video footages can be reported so people can form their own opinions. Just as there's to be truth in advertising, there will be truth in media sources, with the TTT being used where necessary. Violations will result in punishments by the government, and liable and slander suits by people adversely affected. No more "fake News".

SOCIAL SECURITY/HEALTH CARE/WELFARE/UNEMPLOYMENT:

Many people complain about big government and high taxes, yet want or allow the government to provide social security, welfare, food stamps, unemployment and other government handouts, plus even health care. I don't see the logic in that contradictory way of thinking. I feel we have lost sight of the duties we have as members of "the church" and as individuals, have become lazy, and therefore want the government to do everything for us. As stated previously, I don't believe a government should cause its citizens to rely on it rather than God, the church, family, friends, or themselves. Such aforementioned government programs do just that - whereas our families, friends, church, and even private organizations should. So I am opposed to having such government handout programs, and if elected King, I would encourage churches to tend to the needy as they should.

I also don't believe we should have any government funded health care program. I believe in promoting competitive free market enterprise for health insurance, medical care costs, and medications. I would also hire the greatest minds to find inexpensive cures for common diseases as rapidly as possible. I even have some ideas I'd like researched for curing cancer, etc.

As mentioned under "THE ECONOMY/MINIMUM WAGE", I would have strict laws against things like false advertising, fraud and swindling. The 3T would be used on suspected violators. Doing things I stated previously should lower health care, insurance, and medication costs substantially. I'd also encourage churches, private organizations and individuals to do things like: purchase medical coverage for people who need it, form non-profit health insurance plans, and volunteer to provide free or at cost medical care at hospitals, clinics, churches, offices, and doing house calls. I'm also for teaching emergency medical care basics in our Public Education System.

To further lower medical costs, the 3T would be applied in all malpractice lawsuit claims to prevent fraudulent and excessive claims. The 3T would reveal whether the claim was valid, and if so, also aid in determining the extent of malpractice and a FAIR and PRACTICAL compensation. Such usage of the 3T in all aspects of health care would greatly lower costs and hopefully encourage more people to enter the medical fields since there are shortages in the U.S.

If we have any needy citizens who do not have family, friends, the church or private organizations to help them cover expenses and/or remain in their homes, I feel it would be in the country's best interest to create a government funded community in one area for such citizens to go live. The community would have the same Public Education System, plus free housing, food, college and trade courses, and health care. Those able to work would be given jobs within the community and become productive parts of the community in order to cut costs and give them job skills and experience. I would strive to make the community self-sufficient with only a minimal amount of government employees if needed. If we were to have some people with the ability to work who didn't want to do anything to be a productive part of the community, we could vote on what to do with them. Three Biblical options for such lazy people are: forced labor (Prov. 12:24), not feeding (2 Thes. 3:10), and exiling back to the U.S. or some other accepting country (1 Tim. 5:8). Job placement services would be offered so people can leave the community at any time.

As we secede from the U.S., the U.S. government should rightfully reimburse all us former U.S. citizens individual lump sum payments of all the money we already paid individually into Social Security, etc. We can then use or invest that money as we see fit.

Lastly, IF the majority people actually preferred to have a government funded health care program even though it should mean having to pay higher taxes, we would then vote for the program we felt would be best, and I would implement it quickly. That's because under A Democratic Absolute Monarchy (ADAM), THE PEOPLE will have the ultimate say-so, and I as King would be humbly subject to the will of the people in ALL their votings on ANY issues, yet have full authority to put things into effect RAPIDLY! So please vote for me to be King.

With all sincerity and Christianly love,

Bobby Fratta
Polunsky Unit, #999189
3872 FM 350 South
Livingston, TX 77351

This concludes my example of how to campaign.

Now please click onto the appropriate Contents link and ENJOY YOURSELVES!

Congress shall make no law respecting an establishment of religion, or prohibiting the free exercise thereof; **or abridging the freedom of speech**, or of the press; **or the RIGHT of the people peaceably to assemble, and to petition the Government for a redress of grievances.**

July 4, 1776

When in the Course of human events it becomes necessary for one people to dissolve the political bands which have connected them with another and to assume among the powers of the earth, the separate and equal station to which the Laws of Nature and of Nature's God entitle them, a decent respect to the opinions of mankind requires that they should declare the causes which impel them to the <u>SEPARATION</u>.

We hold these truths to be self-evident, that all men are created equal, that they are endowed by their Creator with certain unalienable Rights, that among these are Life, Liberty and the pursuit of Happiness. — That to secure these rights, Governments are instituted among Men, deriving their just powers from the consent of the governed, **— That whenever any Form of Government becomes destructive of these ends, it is the Right of the People to alter or to abolish it, and to institute new Government,** laying its foundation on such principles and organizing its powers in such form, as to them shall seem most likely to effect their Safety and Happiness. Prudence, indeed, will dictate that Governments long established should not be changed for light and transient causes; and accordingly all experience hath shewn that mankind are more disposed to suffer, while evils are sufferable than to right themselves by abolishing the forms to which they are accustomed. But when a long train of abuses and usurpations, pursuing invariably the same Object evinces a design to reduce them under absolute Despotism, it is their right, it is their duty, to throw off such Government, and to provide new Guards for their future security. — Such has been the patient sufferance of these Colonies; and such is now the necessity which constrains them to alter their former Systems of Government. The history of the present King of Great Britain is a history of repeated injuries and usurpations, all having in direct object the establishment of an absolute Tyranny over these States. To prove this, let Facts be submitted to a candid world.

He has refused his Assent to Laws, the most wholesome and necessary for the public good.

He has forbidden his Governors to pass Laws of immediate
and pressing importance, unless suspended in their
operation till his Assent should be obtained; and when so
suspended, he has utterly neglected to attend to them.

He has refused to pass other Laws for the accommodation
of large districts of people, unless those people would
relinquish the right of Representation in the Legislature, a
right inestimable to them and formidable to tyrants only.

He has called together legislative bodies at places unusual,
uncomfortable, and distant from the depository of their
Public Records, for the sole purpose of fatiguing them into
compliance with his measures.

He has dissolved Representative Houses repeatedly, for
opposing with manly firmness his invasions on the rights of
the people.

He has refused for a long time, after such dissolutions, to
cause others to be elected, whereby the Legislative Powers,
incapable of Annihilation, have returned to the People at
large for their exercise; the State remaining in the

meantime exposed to all the dangers of invasion from without, and convulsions within.

He has endeavored to prevent the population of these States; for that purpose obstructing the Laws for Naturalization of Foreigners; refusing to pass others to encourage their migrations hither, and raising the conditions of new Appropriations of Lands.

He has obstructed the Administration of Justice by refusing his Assent to Laws for establishing Judiciary Powers.

He has made Judges dependent on his Will alone for the tenure of their offices, and the amount and payment of their salaries.

He has erected a multitude of New Offices, and sent hither swarms of Officers to harass our people and eat out their substance.

He has kept among us, in times of peace, Standing Armies without the Consent of our legislatures.

He has affected to render the Military independent of and superior to the Civil
Power.

He has combined with others to subject us to a jurisdiction foreign to our constitution, and unacknowledged by our laws; giving his Assent to their Acts of pretended Legislation:

For quartering large bodies of armed troops among us:
For protecting them, by a mock Trial from punishment for any Murders which they should commit on the Inhabitants of these States:

For cutting off our Trade with all parts of the world:

For imposing Taxes on us without our Consent:

For depriving us in many cases, of the benefit of Trial by Jury:

For transporting us beyond Seas to be tried for pretended offences:

For abolishing the free System of English Laws in a neighboring Province, establishing therein an Arbitrary government, and enlarging its Boundaries so as to render it at once an example and fit instrument for introducing the same absolute rule into these Colonies

For taking away our Charters, abolishing our most valuable Laws and altering fundamentally the Forms of our Governments:

For suspending our own Legislatures, and declaring themselves invested with power to legislate for us in all cases whatsoever.

He has abdicated Government here, by declaring us out of his Protection and waging War against us.

He has plundered our seas, ravaged our coasts, burnt our towns, and destroyed the lives of our people.

He is at this time transporting large Armies of foreign Mercenaries to complete the works of death, desolation, and tyranny, already begun with circumstances of Cruelty & Perfidy scarcely paralleled in the most barbarous ages, and totally unworthy the Head of a civilized nation.

He has constrained our fellow Citizens taken Captive on the high Seas to bear Arms against their Country, to become the executioners of their friends and Brethren, or to fall themselves by their Hands.

He has excited domestic insurrections amongst us, and has endeavored to bring on the inhabitants of our frontiers, the merciless Indian Savages whose known rule of warfare, is an undistinguished destruction of all ages, sexes and conditions.

In every stage of these Oppressions We have Petitioned for Redress in the most humble terms: Our repeated Petitions have been answered only by repeated injury. A Prince, whose character is thus marked by every act which may define a Tyrant, is unfit to be the ruler of a free people.

Nor have We been wanting in attentions to our British brethren. We have warned them from time to time of attempts by their legislature to extend an unwarrantable jurisdiction over us. We have reminded them of the circumstances of our emigration and settlement here. We have appealed to their native justice and magnanimity, and we have conjured them by the ties of our common kindred to disavow these usurpations, which would inevitably interrupt our connections and correspondence. They too have been deaf to the voice of justice and of consanguinity. We must, therefore, acquiesce in the necessity, which denounces our Separation, and hold them, as we hold the rest of mankind, Enemies in War, in Peace Friends.

We, therefore, the Representatives of the united States of America, in General Congress, Assembled, appealing to the Supreme Judge of the world for the rectitude of our intentions, do, in the Name, and by Authority of the good People of these Colonies, solemnly publish and declare, That these united Colonies are, and of Right ought to be Free and Independent States, that they are Absolved from all Allegiance to the British Crown, and that all political connection between them and the State of Great Britain, is and ought to be totally dissolved; and that as Free and Independent States, they have full Power to levy War, conclude Peace, contract Alliances, establish Commerce, and to do all other Acts and Things which Independent States may of right do. — And for the support of this Declaration, with a firm reliance on the protection of Divine Providence, we mutually pledge to each other our Lives, our Fortunes, and our sacred Honor.

The following page shows the exact titles and order I intended for each link on the Contents Page. Only 2 forums would be needed for the initial set up. Links 9, 11, 13, and 15 would go to one forum that's to deal with forming New Eden, and links 8, 10, 12, 14 and 16 would go to a second forum that's to deal with forming other new countries. As popularity and donations increase, other forums and links will need to be added and customized to the correlating countries proposed. Again, this site is to be the Central Headquarters for ALL involved in wanting to form ANY new country.

INTENDED CONTENTS FOR WEBSITE

1) Introduction

2) Living in Diversity

3) Form New Countries

4) ADAM Government System

5) New Eden

6) HOW TO: Propose New Countries &/or Government

  Systems &/or Campaign

  to be King, Queen, President, or other

  Leader

7) U.S. 1st Amendment and Declaration of Independence

8) Propose a New Country

9) Propose a New Government System for New Eden

10) Propose a New Government System for Other New

  Countries

11) Campaign to be King, Queen, President, or other

  Leader of New Eden

       As explained in this book's Preface, a website needs to be set up as the

Central Headquarters to get this grassroots movement started so people of all races and religions can get involved easily. As the Copyright claimant/holder of all these writings and concepts, I will give my written consent for everything to be placed onto that site, used in forming an official organization, and also discussed on any Podcast for the organization, FREE OF CHARGE to whichever person(s) I select. I simply want my solution brought to fruition. What's needed now is for all interested persons who are willing and able to: set up a website (with forums and a Donations link — so those who help can be paid), form an official business organization, and/or do podcasts about it all, to please write me at the address below. Please tell me basics about yourself — such as age, sex, religion, race, etc., what you're willing and able to do (your goals and intensions), whether or not you could visit me to discuss details (Note: living in close proximity to Livingston, Texas and visiting me is NOT necessary, but might expedite matters), preferably include one or more photos of yourself, and give me your snail mail and email contacts so I can write you back directly — or thru a friend emailing you for me. If you don't hear back from me, please write me again — as mail does unfortunately get "lost" sometimes.

Thank you and let's get this solution rolling!

Sincerely,

Bobby Fratta

Mailing Address: Robert A. Fratta

Polunsky Unit, #999189

3872 FM 350 South

Livingston, Texas 77351